RAILWAYS

Also in this series

ROBERT BURNS

CLANS AND TARTANS

MARY QUEEN OF SCOTS

PLACE-NAMES

MYSTERIES AND LEGENDS

WILDLIFE

BONNIE PRINCE CHARLIE

CASTLES

FOOD AND DRINK

SCOTCH WHISKY

EDINBURGH

Series editor KENNETH BAILEY
Design by WESTPOINT
Cover photograph by courtesy of The Scottish Tourist Board

© SPURBOOKS
Published by SPURBOOKS (a division of Holmes McDougall Ltd),
Allander House, 137 Leith Walk, Edinburgh EH6 8NS

Printed in Great Britain by Holmes McDougall Ltd, Edinburgh
ISBN 0 7157 2077 5

INTRODUCING SCOTLAND

RAILWAYS

Alastair Smith

Drawings by John Marshall

Spurbooks

CONTENTS

THE GROWTH OF RAILWAYS

THE vital ingredient of a railway is the provision of the track, upon which only specialised vehicles or wagons can be used. Thus the essentials were employed in very ancient times in lands around the Mediterranean Sea, the cradle of civilisation, but were lost to the western world for many centuries. In more recent history, railways were first recorded in the mines of Germany in the mid-sixteenth century.

One hundred years later railways, also known as wagonways, appeared in England, being used for local industrial purposes, principally to convey coals from the mines to the nearest navigable waterway. Such roads as existed were of very low standard, mud baths in winter and during times of flood, but dirt tracks in summer and times of drought.

The Forth and Clyde Canal from Grangemouth on the Forth, to Bowling on the estuary of the Clyde, was opened in 1790 to extend the benefits and cost savings of water transport. But 'Canal Mania' in Scotland was not as extreme as in England. Other canals in central Scotland were the Monkland Canal (near Airdrie), also opened in 1790, the Union Canal (1822), which completed the link from Glasgow to Edinburgh, and the fine-sounding Glasgow, Paisley and Ardrossan Canal which was dug only between Glasgow and Johnstone, and later was used as the basis of a railway line. But canals north of the border never became an integrated network as they did in England and they enjoyed a relatively brief period of pre-eminence. At the time of the canal boom a considerable number of wagonways appeared, including the Alloa wagonway (1768) and the Fordell. The Carron Company near Falkirk also constructed their own wagonway.

Roads, although poor, were still the only means of transport for people. Travel was slow and hazardous; from Glasgow to London in 1750 took three weeks. By 1836, a time when the coaching age was at its peak of perfection, the journey time was reduced to forty-two hours, but was still most uncomfortable!

Early railways used only private ground and were essentially for company or private use. For the later larger railways an Act of Parliament was required which enabled the railway company to acquire, by compulsory purchase if necessary, the land needed for building the permanent way, in a procedure similar to the one laid down for canal construction.

The Kilmarnock and Troon Railway was the first railway in Scotland to have behind it an Act of Parliament. It opened in 1812 and in addition to carrying coals, had a passenger service of sorts by 1817. A Stephenson locomotive is reputed to have been used on the line but it seems to have been a failure, possibly because, being a plate railway with flanged rails of cast iron, it fractured too often to take advantage of steam traction.

From 1826 the growth in small local railways was quite rapid. They included the Monkland and Kirkintilloch Railway, which in 1831 took delivery of the first two locomotives built in Scotland by Murdoch, Aitken and Company of Glasgow. After the success of the Liverpool

The first locomotive to be built in Scotland, 1831

and Manchester Railway many lines opened in Scotland, some in strange places and for no particular purpose. The Glasgow and Garnkirk Railway has the honour of instituting what is generally accepted to be the first regular passenger railway service in Scotland, with four passenger trains daily in both directions.

With the opening of the Glasgow, Paisley, Kilmarnock and Ayr in 1840, and the Glasgow, Paisley and Greenock in 1841, railways began to establish themselves as the most efficient means of transporting the rapidly increasing population. In 1842 the Edinburgh and Glasgow Railway opened for business and whilst mainly on the level, the line required some major civil engineering works, such as the viaduct over the River Almond in West Lothian, still in use on the Inter-City route, and the deep rock cutting into Queen Street Station in Glasgow. This east-west link across the country heralded the Railway Age proper in Scotland which ended the use of canals by passengers.

7

Return train fares for the full journey between Edinburgh and Glasgow ranged from sixteen shillings (80p) First Class to five shillings (25p) for Fourth Class. With the opening of the Caledonian Railway's alternative route via Carstairs a fierce price-cutting war developed and led to the single fare being reduced to sixpence (2½p) by about 1850. Such prices, however, were not to last for long.

After the 1850s the growth of the railway was very rapid. In all a total of 121 companies was granted authorisation by parliament although some, such as the Fochabers and Garmouth Railway and the Glasgow, Strathaven and Lesmahagow Direct Railway, never exercised their powers.

By the 1880s increasing concern for operating methods, the standard of safety and the level of fares, began to improve conditions for travellers. Third Class compartments were fitted with padded seats and the introduction of corridor coaches and dining cars were notable improvements. Nevertheless, by the end of Queen Victoria's reign, the dominance of the railway as the most important means of transport was threatened by the introduction of tramways in the cities and, in Edwardian times, by the introduction of the bus and the increasing use of the private motor car.

During the First World War the railways played a vital role in the movement of men and munitions, not without considerable strain on the individual railway companies. Of great significance was the Government's realisation of the improvements brought about by co-ordinated working, together with the fact that many of the old companies could not afford the vast expense of re-equipping after the wear and tear of war work.

When the railways were decontrolled in August 1921, an Act of Parliament enabled a regrouping and amalgamation of the companies into four main groups. Into the London, Midland and Scottish Railway went the Caledonian, the Glasgow and South Western and twelve smaller Scottish subsidiary companies, while the London and North Eastern Railway absorbed the North British, the Great North of Scotland, and seven smaller Scottish subsidiary companies. This regrouping came into effect on 1 January 1923.

At first, difficulties were encountered because of the many differing designs of locomotives and rolling stock. These, together with the many and varied track standards, eventually led to the introduction of a standard gauge for passenger rolling stock, with a height of 12½ft above rail level and a width of 9¼ft. In addition to the many practical difficulties of railway operations, economic unrest and labour troubles added to the problems, culminating in the National Strike of 1926 when the railways were brought to a halt with the rest of the country.

During the 1930s the railways faced even more severe competition from road transport as well as from the developing airline services. Even before the outbreak of the Second World War in 1939 rail traffic was declining and closures of lines had begun. In this, Scotland suffered more than most other parts of Britain. But it was not all gloom; in 1938 the LNER 4-6-2 *Mallard* hauling seven coaches created a new speed record for steam by reaching 126mph.

By the mid-'30s contingency plans in case of the outbreak of war had been prepared. On the day that war with Germany was actually declared the Railway Executive Committee took charge of the running of the railways on behalf of the Government. By then arrangements for the provision of ambulance trains and evacuation plans were already well in hand. During the war, American-built

The 4-6-0 *Royal Scot class express in the* 1930s

locomotives and those of the 'Austerity' Class designed by
the North British Locomotive Company helped to keep
the railways operating. To discourage unnecessary use of
trains the slogan 'Is your journey really necessary?'
became a familiar part of wartime vocabulary.

When the war ended, restaurant cars soon reappeared
and sleeping cars were re-introduced as well as the travelling post office. With the return of a Labour administ-
ration at the 1945 General Election there followed a programme of nationalisation. As part of this programme the
railways and canals were taken into public ownership.
The British Transport Commission was then faced with
the almost impossible task of restoring the efficiency of the
country's railways.

Between 1948 and 1959 nearly 3,000 miles of track were
closed in an effort to return the railways to a firm financial
footing. Under Dr Richard Beeching's plan *The Reshaping
of British Railways*, line closures and other 'rational-

isations' followed. Some new services such as Freightliner, Motorail and Inter-City were introduced, and to encourage their use a brash new marketing attitude was adopted by British Rail. Another innovation, introduced in 1969, was Rail-Drive, whereby the motorist could take his car with him on long-distance train journeys.

Project XP64 introduced on the *Talisman* service to Edinburgh resulted in the improvement of passenger comfort. The Transport Act of 1968 created other subsidiaries, including the National Freight Corporation and National Carriers Limited. The National Bus Company was also formed. The way forward into the '80s was shown in 1973 when the High Speed Train (HST) set a new diesel-electric speed record of 143mph.

In 1974 the electrification of the London to Glasgow route was completed at a cost of £74 million. The fastest train, the *Royal Scot*, takes five hours for the journey, averaging 80mph. Electrification, with its advantages of fuel economy, and the Advanced Passenger Train (APT) will take the railways in Scotland through to the twenty-first century. Perhaps a new 'Golden Age of the Train' has yet to dawn.

THE BIG FIVE COMPANIES

NORTH BRITISH RAILWAY

THE North British Railway, originally authorised in 1844 to build a railway line from Edinburgh to Berwick upon Tweed, with branch lines to Longniddry and Haddington, was a company which grew up very largely by amalgamation and the incorporation of many earlier railway companies underneath its corporate umbrella. Even before the inauguration of the line between Edinburgh and Berwick in 1846 the company had acquired the Edinburgh and Dalkeith Railway, dating from 1826, for the then very considerable sum of £113,000. The reason for the acquisition of this particular line was that the North British wanted to establish a route from Carlisle through the borders via Hawick to Edinburgh. Such a line was not in fact completed until 1862. A few years later it linked up with the Midland Railway, thus ensuring its financial success.

In a way the Edinburgh-Berwick route was completed before its time because the through route to the south leading to London had to wait until the High Level Bridge at Newcastle over the River Tyne and the Royal Border Bridge spanning the Tweed were completed in 1849-50.

Nevertheless, the company survived and in 1862 grew by amalgamation with the Edinburgh, Perth and Dundee Railway which gave it a foothold north of the Forth. The North British acquired the Edinburgh and Glasgow Railway three years later and so was able to consolidate its position in Glasgow, Fife and the Lothians.

The geographical difficulties presented by the broad Firths of the Tay and the Forth, with the inconvenient train ferry crossings, led to the company's tragic involvement with Thomas Bouch, designer of the Tay Bridge, which featured in a famous railway disaster in 1879. The tremendous and triumphant bridging of the River Forth at Queensferry by a massive cantilever structure designed by Benjamin Baker and John Fowler — the first important bridge to be built in steel rather than cast iron — was begun in January 1883 and completed on 4 March 1890. With these successful links across the Tay and the Forth, the North British was able to operate direct services from Aberdeen, Perth, Dundee and Edinburgh which led to the second round of the Railway Races to the north.

In the 1880s came the proposal by the Glasgow City and District Railway for an underground railway link in Glasgow, the first of Glasgow's underground railways. This section of line completed in 1886 created a circular line on the northern side of the city, with an underground section through the city centre from High Street to Kelvinhaugh, running through the low level station at Queen Street. The Argyle line, opened in 1980 with interchange stations for the present Glasgow Underground system, and other public transport facilities, indicates the continuing validity of the concept.

In Edinburgh, an elegant new station at Waverley and the North British Hotel were completed. The company also began to operate passenger steamers on the Clyde. Many splendid locomotives were developed for the North 13

British, the work of Dugald Drummond being particularly worthy of mention. The position of the North British as the largest of the Scottish companies can be summarised by the following statistics: route miles, 1,378; number of locomotives, 1,107; number of passenger carriages, 3,701; number of freight wagons, 59,972.

CALEDONIAN RAILWAY

The title Caledonian Railway was first used in 1844, perhaps to disguise the fact that backing for the company came mainly from England. The Caledonian was incorporated in July 1845 and it became the premier company of the West Coast Main Line. Construction started in 1845 and by 1847 there were 20,000 men working on the line under the direction of Thomas Brassey. The Carlisle to Beattock Bank section was opened for traffic in September 1847 and passengers completed the journey to either Edinburgh or Glasgow by coach. The first complete rail link to London was on 15 February 1848.

The 'Caley', as it was often known, linked with the lesser Scottish North Eastern and Scottish Midland Junction Railways to give services to Stirling and Perth, and from 1850 a through route from London to Aberdeen. In order to gain a network of railways in the then rapidly developing west of Scotland, the Caledonian gained control of many of the pioneer railway companies in Scotland, including the Glasgow, Garnkirk and Coatbridge, the Clydebank Junction, the Wishaw and Coltness, and the Glasgow and Greenock. The company's first station in Glasgow was at Townhead, but this was later superseded by an extension to Buchanan Street Station in 1849. South of the Clyde, termini were at Bridge Street and South Side Stations.

Caledonian Railway's single-driver engine No 123

In 1867, in order to acquire a port on the east coast the Caledonian purchased the Forth and Clyde Canal to gain access to Grangemouth. Two years later, Central Station in Glasgow was opened with great ceremony as the main station for traffic to the south and the company entered a period of expansion and prosperity. The Callander and Oban Railway opened in 1880; and other projects included the Cathcart Circle. The company also constructed what was then the longest tunnel in Scotland, the 2,800-yd Anderston Cross Tunnel between Glasgow Green and Glasgow Cross. It could also claim the highest railway in Britain, the Leadhills-Wanlockhead branch with a maximum height of 1,498ft above sea level.

The Caledonian reached from Carlisle and Brayton in England, to Glasgow and Edinburgh, and on to Oban, Ballachulish and Aberdeen. It became if not the biggest Scottish railway company, then certainly the most important and most successful, whose holdings included docks 15 and a fleet of steamers which carried countless thousands of Glaswegians 'doon the watter' on the Clyde and on Loch Lomond. Its locomotives were smartly turned out in ultramarine blue lined in black and white, with carriages in crimson lake and wagons brick red.

The Caledonian joined the London, Midland and Scottish Railway in 1923 and contributed to the new company 1,115 route miles, 1,067 locomotives, over 3,000 carriages and 53,300 freight wagons.

GLASGOW AND SOUTH WESTERN RAILWAY

It was just after the peak of 'Railway Mania' in 1850 that the Glasgow, Paisley, Kilmarnock and Ayr amalgamated with the Glasgow, Dumfries and Carlisle to form the Glasgow and South Western Railway, known locally as the 'Sou'West'.

Further amalgamations soon followed: the Ayr and Maybole Junction Railway was acquired in 1856, the Dumfries to Castle Douglas line opened in 1859, and three years later Portpatrick and Stranraer were joined with Castle Douglas to form an important trade route to Ulster. In later years, this section was owned jointly by the Glasgow and South Western and their arch-rival, the Caledonian. In its early years the 'Sou'West' was in reality only a company of limited local importance, but when Carlisle was linked with the south by the Midland Railway in 1865, trade and industry flourished with the opening up of new areas. In 1876 the company opened a splendid new station, St Enoch's in Glasgow, followed by the St Enoch's Hotel in 1879, which set a seal on the company's success.

Much new English-Scottish traffic was generated, but the local character of the railway remained. The company had some fine locomotives; Patrick Stirling, during his period of service from 1853 to 1866 built some excellent 2-2-2s with 6-ft driving wheels, and the North British 'Baltics' in later years also served the company well. The standard locomotive livery was apple green, lined with white and black. The frames were finished in crimson lake to match the carriages, and the goods wagons were a very practical grey.

Although the country across which the railway ran can hardly be described as the most spectacular or difficult in Scotland, the Glasgow and South Western was responsible for two very notable civil engineering works. The first of these was a bank seven miles long, mostly inclined at a gradient of 1 in 67 from Pinwherry southwards, with a deadly 1 in 57 gradient north from New Luce and a fearsome 'swan's neck' S-curve in the middle. The second and more famous landmark is the Ballochmyle Viaduct over the gorge of the River Ayr which has to this day the distinction of being the largest single-span stone-built arch bridge, as well as being the highest, in present-day service with British Rail.

The Glasgow and South Western had a very special place in the west of Scotland and is remembered with great affection. Surprisingly, only one engine used by the company is preserved, No 9, a side-tank locomotive built by the North British Locomotive Company in 1917. It can be seen in Glasgow's Museum of Transport.

In 1923 the 494 route miles, 529 locomotives, 1,600 carriages and over 20,000 wagons of the Glasgow and South Western became part of the London, Midland and Scottish Railway. Now even the impressive edifice of St Enoch's Hotel has gone, victim in 1978 of the demolition worker. The end of an era in railway history, except that a mosaic crest from the hotel has been faithfully reconstructed and is on show in Glasgow's Transport Museum.

HIGHLAND RAILWAY

Formed in 1865 by the amalgamation of the Inverness and Aberdeen Junction, opened in 1858, and the Inverness and Perth Junction, dating from 1863, the Highland Railway covered some of the most romantic and rugged country in the British Isles. From Wick and Thurso in the north, to Kyle of Lochalsh in the west, and to Perth in the Central Highlands (on Caledonian metals), the Highland Railway played a great part in opening up remote areas. As well as servicing the important industries of fishing and forestry, the lines enjoyed a brisk tourist trade in the summer, with 'hunting, shooting and fishing' popular pastimes for the Victorian aristocracy and successful businessmen. The Duke of Sutherland ran his own train *Dunrobin* on the line and had a private station at Dunrobin Castle.

In winter the mainly single track lines of the Highland

Skye bogie of the Highland Railway in winter, 1874

Railway were often the only means of entry into some communities. Very often it was a social need rather than a purely economic one which dictated the operation of the railway. Of the five main Scottish companies, the Highland had the lowest number of locomotives, carriages and wagons per mile of track, but because of the need for powerful engines to haul heavy traffic up steep gradients there evolved in 1894 a series of fifteen 4-6-0 locomotives, the first British designs of this type. The class, numbered 103-117, was built for service on the Perth, Inverness, Wick, Thurso route. Standard livery was 'Stroudley's improved engine green' – a yellow colour! – with red on buffer beams. Carriages were green and sleeping cars varnished teak.

In 1923 the 506 miles of track, 173 locomotives and 3,600 carriages and wagons went to the London, Midland and Scottish Railway.

GREAT NORTH OF SCOTLAND RAILWAY

Incorporated in 1846 to build a railway from Aberdeen to Inverness, but never reaching it, the Great North of Scotland Railway was the only Scottish company to call itself Great, although in fact it was the smallest of the 'Big Five'. But its motto 'The Little But Good' was in some ways justified. One of its most celebrated lines was the Deeside from Ferryhill to Banchory, so often used by Queen Victoria that she had her own special breakfast trolley in Aberdeen Station for bringing food to the train.

Leaving the granite city of Aberdeen and crossing the rich farming lands of the north-east of Scotland, the Great North of Scotland built its own locomotives at Kitty-brewster and Inverurie. It was the only railway in Scotland to be equipped with the electric telegraph throughout its entire length. It also had only First and Third Class carriages. Among its other innovations were the pick up and exchange systems for use in single line working and, in 1896, electric carriage lighting. An electric tramway was operated to the Cruden Bay Hotel in 1899. Possibly its finest piece of engineering was the bow-string bridge over the River Spey about ten miles from Lossiemouth.

At the beginning of the First World War, the Great North of Scotland rebuilt Aberdeen Station in splendid style, something which this vibrant and lively company had in good measure. Before amalgamation, the company livery for locomotives was black with yellow and red lines, but in earlier times it had been green. Carriages were purple with cream tops lined in red and yellow.

When it became part of the London and North Eastern Railway, the Great North of Scotland contributed 335 route miles, 122 locomotives and some 4,500 carriages and wagons.

Great North of Scotland Railway No 49 'Gordon Highlander'

LOCOMOTIVE MANUFACTURE

THE first locomotive used in Scotland, on the Kilmarnock and Troon Railway, was one constructed in the north-east of England by George Stephenson in 1817, but it was not long before home-produced locomotives appeared. The first two Scottish-built locomotives to be put to work were those constructed by Murdoch, Aitken and Company of Glasgow in 1831 for the Monkland and Kirkintilloch Railway. Two years later, in Dundee, the engineering firm of J & C Carmichael built two engines to run on the Dundee and Newtyle Railway, which originally opened with cable and horse traction.

Mitchell and Neilson, later to become Kerr, Neilson and Company, opened their factory in Hydepark Street, Finnieston, Glasgow in 1837 for the purpose of locomotive building. One of the partners, Walter M. Neilson, gradually took control of the firm, which was renamed Neilson and Company in 1848. Expansion continued and by 1861 the works were moved to Springburn, already an important centre for locomotive building, although the name Hydepark Works was retained. The manager of Neilson, Henry Dubs, left in 1863 to found his own company at the Glasgow Locomotive Works at Polmadie. At Neilson,

James Reid became managing director and later sole partner. Neilson himself, however, founded the Clyde Locomotive Company in 1884, and opened premises literally next door to the Hydepark Works in Springburn. But the company was not a success and four years later was sold to Sharp, Stewart and Company, formerly of Manchester. The works was renamed the Atlas Works, and it then prospered.

So the big three Scottish locomotive builders, Neilson Reid, Sharp Stewart, and Dubs came into being. They built not only for the 'Big Five' in Scotland but also for most of the English railway companies. Foreign business was successfully sought and Scottish locomotives were exported to virtually every country aspiring to establish its own railway network. These included, as well as other European countries, Australia, India and South Africa.

By the end of the nineteenth century, Scottish locomotive builders were finding work more difficult to come by: the reason was growing foreign competition. The American firm of Baldwin in Philadelphia had in eight years from 1894 increased its production from 300 to 1,500 locomotives per annum. By 1900 the American domestic market could not on its own absorb these numbers and Baldwin turned its attention to overseas markets. Another challenge came from Germany, who was also seeking to enter traditionally British markets. The importance of locomotive building to Glasgow at this time can scarcely be exaggerated. According to Board of Trade returns for 1899, three-quarters of all the locomotive builders in Britain were located in the Glasgow area.

To face up to the crisis, the three main Glasgow locomotive builders joined forces to form the North British Locomotive Company in 1903. This amalgamation resulted in the largest firm of locomotive builders in Europe, with a work force of 8,000 and a combined works area of sixty acres. But even then their production capacity was only one-third of that of their American rival in the export trade, Baldwin. Even so, the new company got off to a good start. In the first six years of its existence over 400 orders were placed and some 2,400 locomotives designed and built.

After the outbreak of the First World War, two new buildings intended for locomotive construction, subsequently known by the names Mons and Marne, were turned over to the manufacture of weapons. Mons produced over 850,000 high explosive shell-cases while Marne made shell forgings and mines. In addition to some 1,400 locomotives built in wartime at Hydepark, Atlas and Queen's Park Works, torpedo tubes and tanks were also manufactured.

When the war ended, Indian Railways became an important customer, in addition to the home companies such as the North British, Glasgow and South Western and Caledonian. In 1921 three 'Mallet' 0-6-6-0s were ordered for South India and twenty of Gresley's 'Pacifics' were built. Despite this, the three works were not being used to capacity. In 1927 the Atlas Works was closed and put up for sale. The depression in the following years reduced the level of production, even though export orders continued to be received from India, South Africa, Palestine and China. In 1936 the locomotive companies began to make light tanks which had been ordered by the Government.

By the outbreak of the Second World War, total locomotive production in the works since 1903 totalled 8,850, but as in the First World War, hostilities brought tank production to the fore. During the war 143 light tanks and 619 26-ton Matilda tanks were built. Other war work included 1,600,000 bombs and shells, and 13,000 mines. In addition, locomotive production continued: by 1944   23

454 'Austerity' 2-8-0s had been completed.

When peace came there were urgent orders for 110 locomotives for India and 40 metre-gauge 4-6-2s for Malaya. The company diversified and designed and built diesel locomotives called the 'Miner' for underground working. Then followed the North British Shunter with Voith-North British turbo-hydraulic transmission.

In 1953 the company celebrated its fiftieth anniversary with considerable enthusiasm. Yet, in 1955, the entire British locomotive building industry received no share in orders placed by the Indian Railways Board for over 400 locomotives. Japan, Germany, Hungary and Czechoslovakia obtained the bulk of the work. Price was the key factor and it was generally felt that the competition provided by some foreign companies was not entirely fair. For them, it was a matter of underpricing in order to destroy the work-flow of the old established companies in Britain.

The tactic worked, for by 1962 steam locomotive building in Glasgow was a dead industry, and the North British Locomotive Company went into liquidation. Andrew Barclay and Sons acquired the goodwill of the firm, along with plans and archives. Total North British production from 1903 to 1962 was over 11,300 locomotives. The main office block in Springburn became the Springburn College of Further Education, where aspiring engineers continue to be trained.

In addition to the North British, which was by far the biggest Scottish company, there were other firms engaged in locomotive building, although to a lesser degree. The company of Andrew Barclay in Kilmarnock, primarily engineers of mining equipment, found an important niche in the market for industrial shunting locomotives. Some of their engines are still working in Scottish pits. Another industrial locomotive, built in Glasgow by Alexander Chaplin and Company in 1888, which worked in North-

The locomotive works of Andrew Barclay in Kilmarnock

ampton Gas Works for many years, is now preserved in Glasgow's Museum of Transport. Hawthorns of Leith, founded in 1846, supplied a considerable number of locomotives to the North British Railway, and an 0-4-0 tank engine built by them in 1861 is the oldest Scottish-built locomotive to be preserved by the Scottish Railway Preservation Society.

The railway companies themselves were considerable builders of locomotives and mention of them can be found in the list of builders which follows this chapter. Particular mention should be made of the Highland Railway Works at Lochgorm, Inverness and the Great North of Scotland Works, first at Kittybrewster and later at Inverurie, both in Aberdeenshire. They are worthy of note if only for their tenacity in the face of geographical adversity.

The firm of Beardmore was well known in many fields of engineering. Motor cars, armaments, warships, aeroplanes and airships, as well as locomotives, all came from

25

their factories. The locomotive building was the consequence of spare capacity following the First World War. Money was poured into the factory to enable locomotives to be built. The installation of heavy cranes and a steaming shed with friction rollers to enable locomotives to be tested under cover indicated the resolve of Beardmore to succeed in this venture. Nearly 400 locomotives were built by Beardmore at Dalmuir between 1920 and 1931, including the LMS *Prince of Wales* exhibited at the Wembley Exhibition in 1924. The depression reduced demand for new locomotives, and in later years, repairing and rebuilding could do no more than delay the inevitable closure.

By 1963 the steam locomotive was disappearing throughout the world, except in India and China. Even Baldwin in the United States, for decades the greatest locomotive builders in the world, went to the wall. Today's builders are diesel and electrical engineers. Long gone are the traditional craftsmen, but their skills are not quite dead, so long as the enthusiast railway preservation societies continue their sterling work.

LOCOMOTIVE BUILDERS IN SCOTLAND

The following list gives the name of the company, its location and the years during which locomotives were built. Other companies which have at some time been engaged in the building of railway locomotives, but about which there is no firm documentation, have been omitted.

Airdrie Iron Co, Standard Works, Airdrie (c1870-1913)
Allan Andrews & Co, Britannia Engineering Works, Kilmarnock (c1874-82)
Alexander Anderson & Sons, Carfin Boiler Works, Motherwell (c1900)

North British Railway's No 65243 0-6-0 'Maude'

Andrew Barclay, Sons & Co, Caledonia Works, Kilmarnock (1859-present)

Barclays & Co, River Bank Engine Works, Kilmarnock (1872-88)

Barr & McNab, Paisley (1840-54)

William Beardmore & Co, Dalmuir and Parkhead, Glasgow (1920-31)

Blackie & Co, Aberdeen (1848)

Peter Borrie & Co, Tay Foundry, Dundee (c1841)

Caird & Co, Greenock (1840-1)

Caledonian Railway, St Rollox, Glasgow (1854-1928)

J & C Carmichael, Ward Foundry, Dundee (1833)

Alexander Chaplin & Co, Cranstonhill Engine Works, Glasgow (c1860-1900)

Clyde Locomotive Co, Springburn, Glasgow (1886-8)

A F Craig & Co, Caledonia Engineering Works, Paisley (c1870)

W B Dick & Co, Britannia Engineering Works, Kilmarnock (1883-1910)

Dick & Stevenson, Airdrie Engine Works, Airdrie (1864-90)

William Dixon, Calder and Govan, Glasgow (1860-92)

D Drummond & Son, Govan, Glasgow (1891-1900)

Dubs & Co, Glasgow Locomotive Works, Polmadie, Glasgow (1865-1903)

Edinburgh & Glasgow Railway, Cowlairs, Glasgow (1844-65)

Edinburgh, Perth & Dundee Railway, Burntisland, Fife (1861)

Thomas Edington & Sons, Phoenix Iron Works, Glasgow (1840-1)

Forrest & Barr, Glasgow (not recorded)

Glasgow, Paisley & Greenock Railway, Greenock (1846-55)

Glasgow, Paisley, Kilmarnock & Ayr Railway, Glasgow (1845-8)

Glasgow & South Western Railway, Kilmarnock (1851-1921)

Glengarnock Iron & Steel Works, Glengarnock (1913)

Gourlay Bros & Co, Dundee Foundry (not recorded)

Grant Ritchie & Co, Townholme Engine Works, Kilmarnock (1879-1920)

Great North of Scotland Railway, Kittybrewster (1857-1901)

Great North of Scotland Railway, Inverurie (1909-21)

Hawthorns & Co, Leith Engine Works, Edinburgh (1847-c1880)

Highland Railway, Lochgorm, Inverness (1869-1906)

Kilmarnock Engineering Co, Britannia Works, Kilmarnock (1920)

Kinmond, Hutton & Steel, Blackness, Dundee (1838-55)

McCulloch, Sons & Kennedy, Kilmarnock (c1890)

McFarlane, Greenock (no details)

Marshall, Fleming & Jack, Motherwell (c1896)

Martyn Bros, Chapelside Works, Airdrie (c1890)

Monkland & Kirkintilloch Railway, Coatbridge (1840-2)

Murdoch, Aitken & Co, Hill Street Foundry, Glasgow (1831-41)

Neilson & Mitchell, Hyde Park, Glasgow (1843-1903)

North British Locomotive Co, Glasgow (1903-62)

North British Railway, Cowlairs, Glasgow (1865-1924)

North British Railway, St Margaret's, Edinburgh (1856-69)

R Y Pickering & Co, Wishaw (c1900)

Jas M Rowan & Co, Atlas Works, Springburn, Glasgow (1839-51?)

Scottish Central Railway, Perth (1856-66)

Scott, Sinclair & Co, Greenock (1847-9)

Alexander Shanks & Sons, Dens Iron Works, Arbroath (1872-7)

Sharp Stewart & Co, Atlas Works, Springburn, Glasgow (1889-1903)

William Simpson & Co, Aberdeen (1845-53)

A & W Smith & Co, Eglinton Engine Works, Glasgow (c1870)

Stark & Fulton, Glasgow (1839-49)

James Stirling & Co, Dundee (1834-49?)

J & A Taylor, Ayr (1869-71)

Leonard J Todd, Leith (c1870)

John & Thomas Young, Vulcan Foundry, Ayr (c1863)

RAILWAY DISASTERS

S TATISTICS tell us that air travel is the safest form of transportation per passenger mile. The safety record of the railways is also an enviable one, although marred by an accident on the very day that the first passenger railway, the Liverpool and Manchester, was opened. On 15 September 1830, William Huskisson, Member of Parliament for Liverpool, was knocked down by Stephenson's *Rocket* at Parkside, near Newton-le-Willows. Huskisson fractured his thigh and was taken by the *Rocket* to hospital for treatment, but he died later from his injuries.

Major railway disasters in Scotland are mercifully few, but when they happen they have tended to be on a grand and horrific scale. Here is an account of three tragic accidents and one near miss, and to redress the balance, the tragedy of the Tay Bridge disaster is offset by the triumphant story of the building of the Forth Bridge.

TAY BRIDGE DISASTER

For the North British Railway's east coast service, the
Firths of Forth and Tay presented considerable problems.

These were overcome in early years by the use of ferries across the Forth from Granton to Burntisland, a distance of five miles, and across the Tay from Tayport to Broughty Ferry, a distance of two miles.

Civil engineer Thomas Bouch first put forward a proposal for a bridge over the Tay in 1854, but it was not until 1869 that a workable scheme was devised. The bridge would be longer than any previously built; it would cross a wide estuary exposed to fierce gales. After many delays the bridge – nearly two miles of lattice girders on tall pillars – was completed and the first train crossed on 26 September 1877. It was not until 1 June in the following year that fare-paying passengers were carried across the Tay for the first time.

The Tay Bridge gave a great boost to Dundee and to the North British Railway. Queen Victoria crossed the estuary in the royal train on her way to Balmoral, and subsequently knighted Bouch. The bridge, which had cost

The collapse of the Tay Bridge in December 1879

£350,000, was acclaimed a triumph of Victorian engineering.

Then, on 28 December 1879, about 7.30pm on a gloomy Sunday evening during a fierce gale, the high girders collapsed and fell eighty-eight feet into the river below, taking with them the 4.15pm train from Edinburgh with seventy-three passengers and four railwaymen on board: all perished.

The country was stunned by the accident. The Board of Trade enquiry found that the bridge had been badly designed, poorly constructed and maintained, and that Sir Thomas Bouch was mainly to blame. Bouch, a broken man, never recovered from the shock and died within ten months. With him, too, died the plans he had put forward for a bridge across the Firth of Forth. A special North British board meeting, held on the last day of 1879, decided to rebuild the bridge. The new bridge, designed by W H Barlow was opened on 13 June 1887.

The 4-4-0 locomotive which had pulled the fatal train was raised from the scene of the catastrophe, overhauled in Glasgow and put back into service. It then had a macabre nickname, 'The Diver', but it was not until 1908 that it again crossed the new Tay Bridge, nineteen years after the accident. The locomotive was finally scrapped in 1919.

A watch, reputed to have been used by the driver at the time of the disaster, is on show in the Museum of Transport in Glasgow. As a final note to that terrible black Sunday in 1879, the Tay Bridge Disaster was the only major railway accident in Britain in which there were no survivors.

QUINTINSHILL

The worst disaster in the history of British Railways occurred on the Caledonian Railway in Quintinshill, about 1½ miles from Gretna Junction in south-west Scotland, on 22 May 1915. The accident was all the more tragic because it arose from the criminal negligence of two signalmen who, through laziness, had got into the habit of ignoring the safety rules of railway working.

At 6am the signalmen were due to change shifts and the day-shift man, in order to save a journey on foot from Gretna Junction to Quintinshill loop signal-box, used to find out if the 6.10am local train from Carlisle was to put into the side track at Quintinshill to let the Euston to Glasgow express pass. If it was, he would then hitch a lift on the train and arrive slightly late for duty. To complete the deception, the night-shift man instead of making entries in the train register after 6am, would record them on a piece of paper so that his colleague could write them up in his own hand in the proper book.

On that tragic morning, the day-shift signalman managed to hitch a lift on the local train to the signal-box. Because the down siding was occupied by a freight train, the only way to side-track the local train to make way for the express was to reverse it through the cross-over and on to the up line. Paying no attention to safety regulations, this was done. The signalman, busy with the falsification of the train register, then appeared to forget all about the local train. When he was offered a special troop train running from Larbert to Liverpool on the up line, he accepted it and lowered the signals for it to pass. At the same time, the London express was offered from the south, accepted and all signals on the down line cleared for it.

The horrific consequences of this mindless action were inevitable: the troop train, approaching at over 70mph, ran straight into the local train, head on engine to engine, in a violent collision. Such was the force of the impact that the 213-yd train was reduced to a contorted wreck only a third of its original length. Less than a minute later the   33

Euston-Glasgow express, travelling fast and pulled by two engines, ploughed into the wreckage of the crash, running down hapless survivors of the first impact who were helping the less fortunate. Carriages on the troop train were made of wood and, with gas lighting, they became a funeral pyre which burned for more than twenty-four hours.

The official death toll was estimated at 227 with 246 people injured. All except a dozen of the victims were officers and men of the Royal Scots. The enquiry into the accident put most of the blame on the two signalmen, who were subsequently sent to prison for manslaughter. Recommendations were made for the phasing out of gas lighting on trains, for it had been a contributory factor in other railway accidents, and for the adoption of all-steel coaches. Both these recommendations were implemented gradually.

THE CASTLECARY ACCIDENT

At Castlecary, about fifteen miles from Glasgow, on 10 December 1937, an express train from Edinburgh to Glasgow ran into the rear of another express from Dundee to Glasgow while the latter was at a halt.

Weighing in the region of 200 tons, the Edinburgh train forced the Dundee train about fifty yards along the line, seriously injuring its driver. By contrast, the driver of the Edinburgh train was not hurt and his fireman was only slightly injured. The passengers were not so fortunate: thirty-five were killed and 179 injured. Fortunately the coaches were made of steel, for if they had telescoped the accident would have been even more serious. The main cause of the accident was bad visibility of signals caused by the snowstorms.

The accident occured during a heavy snowstorm. The Dundee express was halted at Castlecary by a goods train ahead which found it impossible to run into sidings to clear the main line because points were blocked by snow. The Dundee driver had passed the signals at danger, but stopped again, tragically just out of sight of the signalman in the Castlecary signal box, who believed that the train had continued on its journey. The signalman then accepted the Edinburgh train which, in its turn, also passed the signals at danger in the poor visibility caused by the storm and ran into the rear of the stationary Dundee express.

THE FLOODS OF '48

The south-east of Scotland is normally one of the driest areas of the country, with an average rainfall of about twenty-four inches.

An unlikely setting therefore for a major railway flood incident, but, during the afternoon of 12 August 1948, there occurred over the rolling hills of the Lammermuirs a storm which to this day is still talked about in hushed tones. At Kelso, which was not even the epicentre of the storm, six inches of rain were recorded in less than twenth-four hours. The amount of precipitation at the storm centre is still a matter of speculation.

Little burns, normally insignificant, became raging torrents. The Blackburnrig Burn at Grantshouse became so large that Penmanshiel Tunnel was almost totally engulfed. Near Ayton on the Eye Water, a culvert collapsed and the resulting 'Dam', as the 52-ft embankment was nicknamed, gave great cause for concern. Had the 'Dam' failed, the country town of Eyemouth would, undoubtedly, have been devastated in the manner of 35

The Forth Rail Bridge was opened on 4 March 1890

Lynmouth in Devon a few years later. On the Cock-
burnspath Bank the track had to be realigned.

The twenty-eight miles of track between Berwick and
Dunbar was completely breached on seven bridges and at
three vast landslips. In addition, miles of track foun-
dations and permanent way were weakened.

Work to repair the damage was started almost as soon
as the extent of the potential disaster became known. It is
a tribute to the repair gangs to record that the reconstructed line was opened to goods trains on 25 October
and to the passenger-carrying *Flying Scotsman* one week
later. No lives were lost during the floods, but, ironically,
Penmanshiel Tunnel was the scene of a double fatality
during the late 1970s, during the work to improve the
track to bring it up to the standard required for the
operation of the Inter-City 125 expresses. The tunnel roof
collapsed, killing two men, whose bodies were never
36   recovered, and the tunnel was sealed off.

A BRIDGE ACROSS THE FORTH

Historically, the broad and at times stormy estuary of the River Forth has presented considerable difficulties to the progress of trade in the east of Scotland. Ferry links were established for the use of railway travellers from Granton to Burntisland, and the old Queen's Ferry passage had been operating for centuries.

In 1872, Thomas Bouch advanced a proposal for a bridge across the Forth near the island of Inch Garvie. Parliamentary approval was granted in 1873, and a Forth Bridge Company was formed. A contract was placed for the construction of the bridge but work was delayed until 1879. Late in December of that year, Bouch's Tay Bridge fell and work on his Forth Bridge ceased. Had it been completed it would surely have collapsed as the Tay Bridge had done, for Bouch had allowed for a wind pressure of only 10lb per sq ft, whereas the Board of Trade recommended an allowance of 56lb per sq ft.

The prospect of a bridge over the Forth seemed remote until the idea was revived by Matthew W Thompson, chairman of the Midland Railway, who proposed a joint venture with the North British, the North Eastern and the Great Northern Railways. This idea was favourably received, and Sir John Fowler of the Great Northern and his colleague Benjamin Baker drew up a design for a massive cantilever bridge using the island Inch Garvie as a central base. The recently established naval base at Rosyth, upstream of the site, dictated that a clear headway of 150ft at high spring tide was essential to allow naval vessels to pass beneath the bridge.

In 1882 an Act of Parliament was passed and the contract for building placed with a firm, Tancred, Arrol and Company, especially set up for the construction. Work on the bridge began in January 1883 with the erection of the 37 north and south approaches. The work was on a massive scale, the cost was £3 million, and the number of workmen employed was nearly 5,000. The amount of steel – used for the first time for large-scale bridge construction – totalled 54,160 tons. There were 6½ million rivets needed to join the vast quantity of steel plates. In addition, 740,000 cubic feet of granite, 46,300 cubic yards of rubble masonry and 21,000 tons of cement were used in the construction.

The bridge was completed in 1890 and opened by the Prince of Wales (later King Edward VII), who drove in the last rivet on 4 March 1890. In one sense, work on the bridge is never finished, for to this day a team of twenty painters is employed to paint the steel structure. Seventeen tons of paint are used every year and it takes four years to paint the bridge completely. Total area of steelwork to be painted is 145 acres.

The permanent way is twin-tracked, laid on oak timbers which are fixed longitudinally inside steel troughs. The rails weigh 125 pounds for every yard and they are bolted with coach bolts on to the timbers. The total length of the bridge is 1.57 miles. The height from the top of the main towers to high water mark is 361ft. During construction fifty-seven workmen lost their lives.

From the beginning, the bridge has given sterling service. It survived storm and tempest and even an air raid in the Second World War when the Germans claimed a hit on the bridge, but in fact the smoke that the Germans saw came from a train crossing the bridge and not any direct hit. It is still a vital part of the Inter-City rail link to Dundee and Aberdeen.

JOURNEYS FOR PLEASURE

E VEN in the 1980s, railway journeys can be made
for sheer enjoyment, and sometimes the pleasure
is more in the travelling than in the arrival. There
are two Scottish routes with outstanding attractions and
even those who normally avoid travelling by train have
been known to enthuse about their experience.

WEST HIGHLAND LINE

The West Highland Line, quickly out of Glasgow's Queen
Street Station, soon leaves behind some of the less green
parts of that 'Dear Green Place'. It passes along the north
shore of the Clyde through Dumbarton with its great rock,
to Helensburgh and the Gareloch with its submarine
booms. Then north to Arrochar on Loch Long, the sea
loch, before turning inland to Tarbert on the 'Bonnie,
Bonnie Banks of Loch Lomond'. The railway gives far
greater panoramic views than are usually possible from
the tortuous road along the loch side. On from Ardlui up
Glen Falloch where the gradient through exposed mountain country is 1 in 60, and the maximum speed is 40mph,
with the summit height between Tyndrum and Bridge of   39

The spectacular Glenfinnan viaduct on the Mallaig line

Orchy over 1,000ft. Then across the barren and wind-swept Rannoch Moor with views of four mountains, all over 3,000ft, and superb views all along the line.

The train then descends through Corrour and goes over the viaduct of the rocky River Spean near Tulloch Station, then down the Spean Valley through Roy Bridge, with views to the left of the Monessie. As the train turns to the south-west into Fort William, the scenery is dominated by the massive mound of Ben Nevis, all 4,406ft of it, with patches of snow to be seen at all seasons of the year. The new station at Fort William is the terminus. For those who wish to stay on the train for Mallaig, a distance of forty-two miles, there is the long Glenfinnan viaduct to be seen, possibly the most spectacular on the entire West Highland Line.

Mallaig, at one time the herring capital of Scotland, is the boarding point for the ferry to Armadale on the southern coast of the misty Isle of Skye, across the Sound of

Sleat. Altogether a journey of spectacular scenery, varying from rugged mountains to desolate moorland of grouse and heather, together with memorable glimpses of the magnificent freshwater and sea lochs. A journey which can be a pleasure in any weather or season.

Stations of the West Highland Line

Glasgow (Queen Street), Westerton, Drumchapel, Clydebank, Dalmuir, Kilpatrick, Bowling, Dumbarton, Craigendoran, Helensburgh Upper, Gareloch, Arrochar and Tarbet, Ardlui, Crianlarich, Tyndrum Upper, Bridge of Orchy, Rannoch, Corrour, Tulloch, Roy Bridge, Spean Bridge, Fort William, Banavie, Corpach, Locheilside, Glenfinnan, Lochailort, Arisaig, Morar, Mallaig.

INVERNESS TO KYLE LINE

Travelling on this line, the most remote on British Rail, it is appropriate to recall some comments made over a century ago . . . 'until the coming of the railways and the engineers building them, the British public knew as little about these remote areas as the geographers did about Central Africa twenty years before!' Indeed it is the remoteness and absence of any sign of human interference on the harsh landscape that is the lasting overall impression of the journey to Kyle.

The line, the Dingwall and Skye Railway, was opened to Strome Ferry in 1870, but did not reach Kyle of Lochalsh until 1897. The first nineteen of the line's sixty-four miles give little hint of the splendid isolation that is to follow. Leaving the tidy but uninspiring station at the Highland capital of Inverness, the first notable sight after crossing the River Ness is that most unlikely feature of the Highlands, the Caledonian Canal, now as popular with

41

pleasure sailors as with trawler skippers coming across from the west coast. The line then follows the south shore of the Beauly Firth before turning north after Beauly through Muir of Ord. Here there are views across to the coast of the Black Isle, which is not really an island but one of the most fertile areas of the Scottish mainland. And so to Conon Bridge and Dingwall on the Cromarty Firth, where the Skye line follows the westward arm of the junction, the northerly arm being the former Highland Railway line to Wick and Thurso.

Leaving Dingwall, the single-track railway runs at first through Strath Peffer, under the mound of Ben Wyvis (3,433ft). This is good farming land, with a view south to Strathpeffer, founded as a spa and still popular as a tourist centre, but now without a rail connection. Then past Creag an Fhethick (Raven Rock) on a 1 in 50 gradient by the Falls of Rogie and along the south shore of picturesque Loch Garve to Garve station, the railhead for Loch Broom and Ullapool, where horse-drawn coaches ran until the late 1920s.

Onward and almost due west to the north of Loch Luichart, now like so many lochs in the Highlands harnessed to generate electricity. To Achanalt by lines frequently invaded by sheep, to Achnasheen with road links to Loch Maree – a paradise for anglers – then Glen Torridon and Gairloch, wild lands beloved by climbers. Achnasheen is for many the very essence of the Highlands, where the scent of the heather mingles with that of the peat and the pines. The line now turns south-west, by Strath Carron to Loch Carron, a sea loch with the track plunging through each successive hillock in a vertical rock-cutting. Next is Strome Ferry and its once bustling harbour from which, in times past, Highland Railway steamers departed for Portree on Skye and Stornoway on the Isle of Lewis.

The final few miles of the Kyle extension are through very typical West Highland scenery of mountain, silted-up river valley, coastal flat and deep sea loch, past the much photographed village of Plockton. It is hard to believe that the trip from Inverness takes only three hours, such is the variety of the scenery witnessed. Of Kyle it is really not too unkind to say that the best thing is the view to Skye, with the Cuillins forming a magnificent backdrop – that is, as many slightly disappointed tourists would point out, when they can be seen through the mists.

For those who wish to step on to Skye, frequent ferry services across the fast flowing Kyle to Kyleakin take only a few minutes – a short crossing but a memorable one. For those not returning the same day, the hotel run by the British Transport Hotels offers excellent accommodation and views. Truly a fitting place to conclude one of the great railway journeys of this country.

A word of advice however for those tempted by either of these two great travel spectaculars – do it soon – the opportunity may disappear forever if the chilly winds of recession blow for much longer. And lastly, take your camera and a spare film or two to capture for yourself the scenic splendour of these railways for pleasure.

Stations from Inverness to Kyle of Lochalsh

Inverness, Muir of Ord, Dingwall, Garve, Lochluichart, Achanalt, Achnasheen, Achnashellach, Strathcarron, Attadale, Stromeferry, Duncraig, Plockton, Kyle of Lochalsh.

A RAILWAY MISCELLANY

THE RAILWAY RACES

B Y the 1880s, Victorian Britain had become accustomed to a complete network of railway routes throughout the land. The railway companies vied with each other to bring greater comfort and safety to the travelling public. Third Class travel was introduced on express train services. Luxury coaches, known as Pullmans after their American inventor, George Mortimer Pullman, were used on various routes from 1874, including the destinations of Glasgow and Edinburgh. Regular sleeping car coaches for First Class travellers were inaugurated by Scotland's largest railway company, the North British. Refreshment carriages, or 'hotel cars' were introduced, and to the great relief of all travellers, corridor trains with toilets became commonplace, although, as the notice says, 'not while the train is standing in the station'.

The greatest manifestation of rivalry between the companies showed itself in the Railway Races to the north. Speeds on Britain's iron roads were already the highest in the world. Early in 1888 the 'Special Scotch Express' took nine hours for the 395-mile King's Cross to Edinburgh

(Waverley) run. By August the time had been reduced to 7hr 27min, in spite of the obligatory 'lunch stop' of twenty minutes at York, and the average speed was 57.7mph. On the west coast, the London and North Western and the Caledonian Railways improved timings over their 400-mile route with journey times of 7hr 6min, at an average speed of 56.2mph.

One of the most celebrated locomotives to take part in the first 'Race to the North' was the Neilson-built single-driver express engine No 123 of the Caledonian Railway. A unique locomotive, it was built in only sixty-six days so that it could be exhibited at the International Exhibition of Industry, Science and Art in Edinburgh in 1886. After its part in the Railway Races, when it completed 100¾ miles in 102 minutes, Locomotive No 123 frequently made two round trips daily between Glasgow and Carlisle over the notorious Beattock Bank (1016ft) a daily total of some 409 miles. No 123 was the last single-driver to be steamed

Caledonian locomotive designed by Dugald Drummond, 1884   45

in Britain and is now preserved in Glasgow's Museum of Transport.

There was much rivalry between the night expresses on the west and east coast routes to Scotland, which was heightened by the fact that the rival trains ran over the same metals from Kinnaber Junction to Aberdeen, a distance of some 38 miles. The signalman at Kinnaber was the sole arbiter of which train should take precedence if both arrived at the same time; this did happen once and the 'Caley' signalman sportingly gave priority to the North British train.

The 'Race to Aberdeen' was a sequel to the opening of the Forth Rail Bridge, which shortened the east coast route and allowed the King's Cross train to reach Aberdeen a quarter of an hour ahead of the Euston train. Then came the announcement that as from 1 July 1895 the west coast train from Euston would arrive only five minutes later than the east coast train. A further cut of fifteen minutes on the east coast route was promptly announced and the race was well and truly on. One cut followed another until two trains were running on the west coast, the 'racer', and the 'follower' which did the intermediate stops.

The climax came on the night of 22-23 August 1895, when the west coast train, leaving Euston at 8pm, arrived in Aberdeen at 4.32am, travelling 540 miles in 512 minutes, including stops at Crewe, Carlisle and Perth, at an incredible average speed of 63.3mph.

Sanity prevailed, and by mutual agreement the races were ended and schedules agreed; journeys on the east coast taking 10hr 25min from London, and on the west coast just five minutes more. An exciting chapter in railway rivalry had come to a close: the real winner of the races was the passenger who benefited greatly from improved journey times.

THE BENNIE RAILPLANE

Eugen Langen patented a monorail system in Germany at the end of the nineteenth century. A monorail device invented by George Bennie in Scotland enjoyed a brief burst of glory in the 1930s. His experimental railplane track, 426 feet in length was built above the LNER line at Milngavie, near Glasgow.

The railplane employed the reverse principle of the conventional locomotive. Instead of relying on adhesion for tractive effort it used its wheels only as guides, motive power being provided by aircraft propellers. The test line opened on 8 July 1930. The car was built by Arrol-Johnston and Aster Engineering at Dumfries, except for the ends and bogies which were made by Mirlees Watson, Glasgow. The two specially designed electric motors, each rated 60bhp at 1,200rpm, were manufactured in Norwich, the propellers by Airscrews Limited, Weybridge. The steelwork, with steel trestles at 80-ft intervals, was by the Teeside Bridge and Engineering Company, Middlesbrough. The car was streamlined, and should have been capable of 120mph.

Bennie, who lived at the Central Hotel when in Glasgow, had invested £150,000 of his own money in his railplane. He attracted wide publicity and various schemes were suggested, including a railplane track above the Edinburgh-Glasgow main line, and a 500-mile planeway between Djibouti and Addis Abbaba, a proposal that was ended by the Abyssinian War. Another scheme considered was a railplane link between Blackpool and Southport. But all projects for the railplane were shelved at the outbreak of the Second World War.

Throughout the war years Bennie continued to improve his system, and late in 1946 a new company was formed, the George Bennie Airspeed Railway. This company

47

bought the world rights to the Bennie system, but successive yearly reports told the same sad story – 'no trading has taken place'.

Bennie died in obscurity in 1954 and the George Bennie Airspeed Railway Company was dissolved late in 1956. The railplane, abandoned, mouldered in a field near Milngavie until the 1960s when it was sold for scrap. The railplane miracle of 1930 was dead, if indeed it had ever been alive.

A model of the railplane survives in Glasgow's Museum of Transport and with a few fleeting seconds of cine film in the possession of the Scottish Film Council, is the only tangible evidence of a Scottish railway enterprise once thought promising.

THE GLASGOW UNDERGROUND

The Glasgow Underground, or the Subway as it was affectionately known by generations of Glaswegians, was opened by the Glasgow District Subway Company on 14 December 1896. The trains were then cable-hauled, the winding house being in Scotland Street. There were fifteen stations on the 6.56-mile circular route, with trains operating in both directions in twin tunnels 11ft in diameter. The gauge of the track was 4ft, and island platform stations served both tracks.

The motor coaches, driven by the driver or 'gripman' were connected to the continuously moving cable by the 'gripper', which was disengaged to allow the train to stop in the station. The cable speed was 15mph. The system proved very popular and soon the gripper cars pulled trailer cars round the system. A total of sixty coaches was used on the subway; the gripper coaches were built by the Oldbury Railway Carriage and Wagon Company, Bir-

The Glasgow Underground before its modernisation in 1979

mingham and the trailer coaches by Hurst Nelson and Company, Motherwell.

From its earliest days, the subway was in competition with the Corporation-owned trams, and following the First World War the private company entered long negotiations which resulted in the subway being purchased by the Corporation Tramways Department on 1 August 1923.

The system continued virtually unaltered, except for a change in livery from the rich plum of the Glasgow District Subway to Corporation red, for the next ten years. Following an official inspection of the system on 6 March 1933, it was decided that the whole system should be electrified, using existing rolling stock. After receiving tenders from outside firms, the Corporation undertook the work themselves. This was completed by 1935.

The Second World War was one of the busiest times for the subway, taking many thousands of workers to the

49

Clyde shipyards where they played such a vital part in the war effort. Unlike the London Underground the Glasgow Subway could not be used as an air-raid shelter because it was not deep enough to afford adequate protection. The subway was put out of action by enemy activity on 18 September 1940, but was back in business by the following January.

By the 1960s the fleet of cars was long past its expected working life but, with the demise of the Glasgow tram in 1962, a 'fresh' infusion of electric motors and traction parts cannibalised from the tramcar fleet kept this remarkable museum piece of Victorian engineering in operation.

In 1975, as part of the Scottish local government reform, the subway was taken over by the Greater Glasgow Passenger Transport Executive and, despite mounting engineering difficulties, continued to run until 21 May 1977, when it was closed for modernisation, somewhat prematurely because of a roof fall.

The revamped subway was officially inaugurated by HM Queen Elizabeth on 1 November 1979 and opened to the public on Wednesday 16 April 1980. The new coaches, constructed by Metropolitan Vickers in Birmingham and finished in bright orange have already been nicknamed 'Clockwork Oranges' by the Glasgow public, but for many of the older generation the red 'wee trains' are the real Glasgow Underground.

A reconstruction of Merkland Street Station showing preserved rolling stock of the Glasgow District Subway and Glasgow Corporation can be seen in Glasgow's Museum of Transport.

LOCOMOTIVES PRESERVED

COMPARED with locomotive preservation in England, most Scottish efforts seem somewhat minor, but this is due as much to the geography of the country and the relatively low density of population as to any lack of enthusiasm. The undernoted organisations are to the forefront of railway preservation.

It should be remembered that museums and societies are constantly adding to their collections and that the locomotive lists may well be out of date by the time you read them. The details of preserved locomotives give the type, date of manufacture, the builder and the customer.

ROYAL SCOTTISH MUSEUM

Founded in the 1850s, this national museum houses the oldest surviving locomotive anywhere in the world. It dates from 1813 and was built by William Hedley for Wylam Colliery, not far from Newcastle upon Tyne, and was once used as a power source for a boat on the River Tyne. 'Wylam Dilly' worked at Wylam until 1862 when it was transferred to Craghead Colliery. Later it was exhibited at the Edinburgh Exhibition of 1886 and thereafter went to the Royal Scottish Museum. Other notable locomotives in the national collection are at present operated by the Scottish Railway Preservation Society. The museum is situated in Chambers Street in Edinburgh not far from Waverley Station and is open all year round (except for Christmas Day and 1 January).

Locomotives preserved

0-4-0 Wylam Dilly (1813) Built by William Hedley for Wylam Colliery.

4 wheel 2ft 6in gauge (1902) Built by Baldwin, Philadelphia, United States for Oakland Oil Co, Winchburgh.

4 wheel overhead electric (1908) Built by British-Thomson-Houston for Caldina Port Power Station, Dundee.

MUSEUM OF TRANSPORT, GLASGOW

Situated in the former Glasgow Corporation Tramworks and adjacent to Pollokshields East Station is Glasgow District Council's Museum of Transport. One of the most comprehensive transport museums anywhere in Britain, the museum houses examples of locomotives of all the big five Scottish railway companies. Included in the collections are the famous Neilson-built Caledonian No 123, the last single-driver to run in the UK, and the only survivor of the Glasgow and South Western Railway, a 0-6-0-tank built in 1917. The museum's address is 25 Albert Drive, Glasgow G41 2PE and it is open all year round (except Christmas Day and 1 January).

Locomotives preserved

4-2-2 No 123 (1886) Built by Neilson & Co, Hydepark, Glasgow for Caledonian Railway.

'Wylam Dilly', the world's oldest surviving locomotive

0-6-0 No 9 (1917) Built by North British Locomotive Co, Hydepark, Glasgow for Glasgow and South West Railway.

4-4-0 No 256 (1913) Built by North British Railway Co, Cowlairs, Glasgow for North British Railway.

4-6-0 No 103 (1894) Built by Sharp, Stewart and Co, Atlas Works, Glasgow for Highland Railway.

4-4-0 No 49 (1920) Built by North British Locomotive Co, Hydepark, Glasgow for Great North of Scotland Railway.

0-4-0 TG No. 2368 (1888) Built by Alexander Chaplin and Co, Anderston, Glasgow for Northampton Gas Works.

STRATHSPEY RAILWAY

Operated by the Strathspey Railway Company, this private railway at present runs over a $5\frac{1}{4}$-mile track of the old Highland Railway, which was closed in the early 1960s. The line has also received financial assistance from the Highlands and Islands Development Board in recognition of its important contribution to tourism. In addition to the magnificent scenery, the passenger making the journey from Speyside Station at Aviemore to Boat of Garten has the chance to see one of the famous Loch Garten ospreys. For the future there is the possibility of an extension of the railway to Grantown on Spey which would give a track of nearly thirteen miles. Enquiries to the Strathspey Railway, The Station, Boat of Garten, Inverness-shire PH24 3BH. At present the railway operates from mid-May to mid-October.

Locomotives preserved

4-6-0 No 5025 (1934) Built by Vulcan Foundry for London, Midland and Scottish Railway.

0-6-0 No 828 (1899) Built by Caledonian Railway, St Rollox, Glasgow for Caledonian Railway.

2-6-0 No 46464 (1950) Built by British Railways, Crewe for British Railways.

0-6-0 ST No 3686 (1948) Built by Hunslet Works for National Coal Board, Durham Area.

0-6-0 ST No 2864 (1943) Built by Hunslet Works for National Coal Board, Backworth.

0-6-0 ST No 7097 (1943) Built by R Stephenson and Hawthorn for National Coal Board, Backworth.

0-6-0 T No 3017 (1935) Built by Barclay, Kilmarnock for Wemyss Private Railway.

0-4-0 ST No 2315 (1951) Built by Barclay, Kilmarnock for SSEB, Braehead.

0-4-0 ST No 2073 (1939) Built by Barclay, Kilmarnock for Scottish Malt Distillers.

0-4-0 ST No 2020 (1936) Built by Barclay, Kilmarnock for Scottish Malt Distillers.

0-4-0 ST No 1890 (1926) Built by Barclay, Kilmarnock for Edinburgh Gas Works.

LOCHTY PRIVATE RAILWAY

The main attraction on this little private railway owned by local farmer Mr John Cameron, is the former LNER Coronation Class A4 Gresley Pacific No 60009 *Union of South Africa* and such is the enthusiasm for the locomotive that visitors have come to this quiet corner of the Neuk of Fife from all over the world. Thanks to the enlightened attitude of British Rail with regard to the operation of steam locomotives on their metals this former 100-mph locomotive can still be found hauling special excursion trains from time to time. The Lochty Private Railway is open from mid-June to early September and is located off the B940 from Cupar to Crail in this picturesque part of Fife.

Locomotives preserved
0-6-0 No 16 (1944) Built by Bagnall.
0-4-0 (1915) Built by Peckett.
4-6-2 *Union of South Africa* No 60009 (1937) Built by Doncaster Works for London and North Eastern Railway.

SCOTTISH RAILWAY PRESERVATION SOCIETY

Founded some twenty years ago the Scottish Railway Preservation Society offers to its members the chance to work on the maintenance of Scotland's largest collection of historic locomotives, coaches and wagons. For many years without a track of its own, it now seems likely that a site at Bo'ness in the shadow of the Forth Bridges will allow this wide ranging collection to be shown to its best advantage. The yard at Wallace Street, Falkirk is usually open at weekends at a nominal charge, but the arrangements regarding Bo'ness have not to date been finalised. As well as its own collections the Society has locomotives such as the former LNER 4-4-0 *Morayshire* and *Ellesmere* by Hawthorns of Leith built in 1861 and on loan from the national collection. In addition the Society is usually able to organise 'specials' over British Rail metals. Enquiries to Scottish Railway Preservation Society, Wallace Street, Falkirk FK2 7DR.

Locomotives preserved

4-4-0 *Morayshire* (1927) Built at Darlington for London and North Eastern Railway.

2-6-4T No 80105 (1955) Built at British Railways, Brighton for British Railways.

0-4-4T No 419 (1907) Built by Caledonian Railway, St Rollox, Glasgow for Caledonian Railway.

0-6-0 No 65243 *Maude* (1892) Built by Neilson and Co., Hydepark, Glasgow for North British Railway.

0-6-0T No 1 *Lord Roberts* (1902) Built by Neilson Reid, Glasgow for Coltness Iron Co.

0-6-0T No 20 (1939) Built by A Barclay for Wemyss Private Railway.

0-4-0 ST No 13 *Kelton Fell* (1876) Built by Neilson and Co, Hydepark, Glasgow for North British Railway.

0-4-0 ST No 3 (1928) Built by A Barclay for Clyde Valley Electrical Power Co.

0-4-0WT *Ellesmere* (1861) Built by Hawthorn, Leith for Howe Bridge Colliery, Wigan.

4wWE *Fairfield* 150hp (1940) Built by English Electric for Fairfield Shipbuilding and Engineering Co.

EVENTS IN RAILWAY HISTORY

This list details some of the important events in railway history generally, but with particular reference to Scotland.

1722   Opening of the Tranent-Cockenzie Wagonway (with wooden rails) near Edinburgh, probably the first railway in Scotland.

1765   James Watt, instrument-maker at Glasgow University, improves the efficiency of Newcomen's steam engine and is granted a patent in 1769.

1804   First steam railway locomotive built by Richard Trevithick.

1808 (27 May)   Incorporation of the first railway in Scotland, the Kilmarnock and Troon. The line opened in 1812 with horses providing the motive power. Steam traction was introduced in 1817.

1825   (27 Sep)   Opening of Stockton and Darlington Railway. Stephenson's *Locomotion* used on opening journey, but passenger trains were hauled by horses.

1826   Monkland and Kirkintilloch Railway opens. Horse and steam traction used.

1829   The Rainhill Trials. Stephenson's *Rocket* wins £500 prize.

LMS Travelling Post Office, c1840-50

1830 (15 Sep) Liverpool and Manchester Railway opens. The first public railway to carry passengers and other traffic by steam power.

1831 First locomotives built in Scotland by Murdoch, Aitken & Co.

1831 Opening of Glasgow and Garnkirk Railway.

1831 (21 Sep) Opening of Dundee and Newtyle Railway. At first cable and horse but later (1833) steam.

1838 (6 Oct) Opening of Dundee and Abroath Railway.

1839 Bradshaw's first railway timetable appeared. The last was published in 1961.

1840 (12 Aug) Completion of the Glasgow, Paisley, Kilmarnock and Ayr Railway.

1842 (21 Feb) Opening of Edinburgh and Glasgow Railway (Haymarket and Queen Street Stations).

1842 Queen Victoria makes first railway journey, giving royal approval to railway travel.

1844 Railway Act makes it compulsory to provide Third Class carriages. The fare – one penny (1d) per mile.

1845   The Gauge Commission is formed to decide on the 'Battle of the Gauges'. Stephenson's standard gauge is adopted.

1846 (18 Jun)   North British Railway opens line between Edinburgh and Berwick.

1846 (22 Jun)   Foundation of Caledonian Railway. In 1848 has lines Glasgow-Carstairs-Lockerbie-Carlisle and Carlisle-Carstairs-Edinburgh.

1847-8   Caledonian opens Carlisle-Beattock-Glasgow links.

1848 (22 May)   Scottish Central Railway opens Perth-Stirling line.

1848 (2 Aug)   Scottish Midland Junction Railway links Perth and Forfar.

1849   Edinburgh and Hawick Railway opens.

1849 (1 Nov)   Buchanan Street Station, Glasgow, opens.

1850 (1 Apr)   Aberdeen and London linked by rail.

1850 (29 Aug)   Berwick Royal Border Bridge completes London-Edinburgh lines.

1850 (28 Oct)   Amalgamation of railways to form the Glasgow and South Western Railway.

1854 (12 Sep)   Opening of first section of Great North of Scotland line.

1855 (5 Nov)   Inverness and Nairn Railway opens.

1856 (7 Apr)   Perth and Dunkeld Railway opens.

1859   Pullman introduces sleeping car service in United States.

1860 (7 Nov)   Dumfries and Castle Douglas Railway opens.

1861 (12 Mar)   Portpatrick and Wigtownshire Joint Railway opens.

1862 (11 Jun)   Inverness and Ross-shire Railway opens line to Dingwall.

1863 (Jan)   Opening of world's first underground railway (part of Metropolitan Railway).

1863 (9 Sep)   Inverness and Perth Junction Railway opens.

1869 (8 Jul)   Caledonian Railway opens Glasgow-Edinburgh line via mid-Calder.

1869 (23 Dec)   Glasgow and South Western Railway links with Greenock.

1870   Dingwall and Skye Railway reached Strome Ferry. It did not get to its ultimate destination, Kyle of Lochalsh, until 1897.

1874   Pullman cars introduced by Midland Railway.

1874 (28 Jul)   Sutherland and Caithness Railway links Highland Railway system to Wick and Thurso.

1876 (17 Oct)   St Enoch's Station, Glasgow opens. It was closed in 1966 and demolished in 1978.

1878 (1 Jun)   Tay Bridge opens, longest railway bridge in the world.

1878 (28 Dec)   Tay Bridge disaster, seventy-eight killed.

1879 (1 Jul)   Caledonian Railway opens Glasgow Central Station.

1880 (1 Jul)   Callander and Oban Railway completed.

1885 (1 Jul)   Mail only service introduced, London-Aberdeen.

1887 (13 Jun)   New Tay Bridge opened.

1888   'Race to the North' competition between east and west coast routes bring improvements to Anglo-Scottish services.

1890 (4 Mar)   Forth Bridge opens.

1895 (22 Aug)   'Race to Aberdeen' between east and west coast routes.

1896 (14 Dec)   Glasgow District Subway opens.

1900 (1 Aug)   Dining cars and corridor coaches on *Flying Scotsman*. No 'lunch interval' at York.

1914   Railways taken over by Government on outbreak of First World War.

1915 (22 May)   Britain's worst rail accident at Quin-

A 4-6-2 Gresley Pacific hauls the 'Flying Scotsman'

tinshill on Caledonian Railway, 227 killed.

1917 (12 Dec)   World's worst railway accident, in France, 543 killed.

1923 (1 Jan)   Amalgamation of 123 railway companies into four groups, London, Midland and Scottish; London and North Eastern; Great Western; and Southern.

1924 (Jun)   Gleneagles Hotel, Perthshire opens.

1928   All-steel car trains introduced by LNER.

1938 (3 Jul)   LNER *Mallard* creates new record for steam train of 126mph.

1939 (13 Aug)   Automatic Train Control (ATC) on LNER Glasgow-Edinburgh line.

1939   Minister of Transport appoints Railway Executive Committee to run railways during Second World War.

1945 (1 Oct)   Restaurant car services restored on LMS, LNER and SR.

1947 (6 Aug)   Royal Assent for Transport Act 1947 establishes British Transport Commission.

1948 (1 Jan)   Railways in Britain are nationalised.

1949 (Jun)   Diesel locomotives run non-stop from London (Euston) to Glasgow.

1952 (8 Oct)   Rail disaster at Harrow, Middlesex, 112 killed.

1956 (Jun)   Third Class redesignated Second Class.

1958 (13 Feb)   Battery rail car introduced on Aberdeen-Ballater line.

1960 (18 Mar)   *Evening Star* last named steam locomotive to be built for British Railways. Now preserved in York.

1960 (7 Nov)   Glasgow electric 'Blue Trains' introduced.

1963 (1 Jan)   Dr Beeching becomes Chairman of Railways Board.

1965   Change of name to British Rail.

1967 (5 Jun)   Glasgow suburban electric services extended to Gourock and Wemyss Bay.

1968   Experimental Advanced Passenger Train introduced.

1973   High Speed Train reaches 131mph.

1974   Electrification of Glasgow-Crewe line.

1975   150th anniversary of Stockton and Darlington Railway.

1977 (21 May)   Closure of 'old' Glasgow Underground for modernisation.

1980 (16 Apr)   Re-opening of 'new' Glasgow Underground to public.

READING LIST

Casserley, H C, *Observer's Book of British Steam Locomotives*, Warne

Casserley, H C, *Preserved Locomotives*, Ian Allan

Cross, D, *The Last Decade of Scottish Steam*, Bradford Barton

Glen, Glen & Dunbar, *Great North of Scotland Railway Album*, Ian Allan

Glen, Glen & Dunbar, *Caledonian Cavalcade*, Ian Allan

Marshall, John, *The Guinness Book of Rail Facts and Feats*, Guinness Superlatives

Nock, O S, *Railway Archaeology*, Patrick Stephens

Nock, O S, *British Steam Locomotives in Colour*, Batsford

Smith, D L, *Legends of the Glasgow & South Western Railway in LMS Days*, Bradford Barton

Thomas, John, *Regional History of the Railways of Great Britain (Vol 16), Scotland, The Lowlands and the Borders*, David & Charles

Thomas, John, *The West Highland Railway*, David & Charles

Thomas, John, *The Skye Railway*, David & Charles

Thomas, John, *The Scottish Railway Book*, David & Charles

INDEX